Way of the Warrior

# NINJAS

## Masters of Stealth and Secrecy

Joanne Mattern

Children's Press®
A Division of Scholastic Inc.
New York / Toronto / London / Auckland / Sydney
Mexico City / New Delhi / Hong Kong
Danbury, Connecticut

Book Design: Elana Davidian and Michael DeLisio
Contributing Editor: Eric Fein
Photo Credits: Cover © Werner Forman/Art Resource; pp. 5, 8, 19, 22, 33, 40
Christopher Logan; pp. 7, 28, 39 © Michael S. Yamashita/Corbis; p. 11 © Alinari
Archives/Corbis; p. 15 © Corbis; p. 16 © Sakamoto Photo Research Labora/Corbis;
p. 24 © Royalty-Free/Corbis; pp. 26, 31 © Horace Bristol/Corbis; p. 35 © Asian Art
& Archaeology, Inc.; p. 37 © Ric Ergenbright/Corbis

Library of Congress Cataloging-in-Publication Data

Mattern, Joanne, 1963–
    Ninjas : masters of stealth and secrecy / Joanne Mattern—1st ed.
    p. cm. — (Way of the Warrior)
    Includes index.
    ISBN 0-516-25120-1 (lib. bdg.) — ISBN 0-516-25089-2 (pbk.)
    1. Ninja—Juvenile literature. I. Title. II. Series.

    UB271.J3M38 2005
    355.5'48—dc22
                                                        2004006458

1 2 3 4 5 6 7 8 9 10 R 14 13 12 11 10 09 08 07 06 05

# Contents

# INTRODUCTION

In the dead of night, a small band of men makes its way toward a castle. The castle is the home of a military leader known as a warlord. A rival warlord has hired these men to capture the castle. It will not be easy. The castle has high walls that are impossible for ordinary men to climb. But these are not ordinary men. These men are ninjas, masters of stealth and secrecy. Using special climbing tools, the band of men quickly and quietly scales the wall.

Once over the wall, the ninjas sneak into the castle. No one sees or hears them. In the main hall of the castle, they start a large fire. The fire is a signal to fellow ninja warriors who are hiding in the surrounding woods. These ninjas quickly attack the castle. Their attack catches the warlord of the castle and his army by complete surprise. The warlord's army becomes confused and stunned by the quickness and fighting ability of the ninjas. The warlord surrenders. Once again, the ninjas have proven themselves in combat.

The art of stealth or *nonuse* was used by ninjas. It is believed to have been passed down from mystic priests. These priests needed to protect themselves from Japan's ruling class.

From around the twelfth through the seventeenth centuries, ninjas were Japan's famous warriors. During this time, they developed a reputation as mysterious spies and deadly fighters. Their history is a fascinating mix of fact and fiction. Let's pull back the curtains of time and explore the ways of the ninjas—Japan's shadowy warriors.

Even a fortress as strong as Osaka Castle, which was surrounded by well-guarded walls, could be successfully attacked by ninjas.

# CHAPTER ONE

# The Secret Beginnings of the Ninjas

## Common Beliefs About Ninjas

Most of us think of ninjas as warriors dressed in black, armed with lethal weapons and magical powers. This is partly true. Ninjas *did* dress in special black clothing. They did that only at night, when they did not want to be seen. During the day, they wore other types of clothing to fit their mission. For example, suppose they were spying on an enemy in a crowded marketplace. In this case, ninjas would dress like the people in the market to blend in with the crowd.

Techniques such as the sweeping step allowed the ninja to move unnoticed over wooden planks, narrow beams, or straw matting.

Ninjas had many skills and abilities that made them *seem* magical. But it was their intense physical and mental training that created this impression. Most people living during the time of the ninja feared what they did not understand. These people made up stories about ninjas having magical powers. Ninjas were happy to let these stories spread. It made them appear more threatening to their enemies.

## Early Japan

Ninjas were active in Japan from around the 1100s to the 1600s. During this time, Japan was ruled by a military leader called a shogun. The shogun used warlords to help him control Japan. Each warlord owned land. The warlords were constantly at war with each other to gain more power and land.

To protect them from enemy attacks, warlords used warriors called samurai. The samurai also protected poor farmers who worked for the warlords. The warlords gave samurai land in payment for their loyalty

Toshugawa Yoshinobu was Japan's last shogun. This photograph of him was taken in the 1860s.

and protection. This system of giving land and protection in return for work and loyalty was known as feudalism.

The samurai followed a special code of honor. This code prevented them from spying or doing other things that were thought to be dishonorable. But the samurai were not the *only* group of warriors in Japan at this time. The other group lived by no such code of honor. They simply did what their masters asked of them. These were the ninjas.

## Land of the Ninja

No one is exactly certain when ninjas first appeared. Most researchers agree that the birthplace of the ninja is the island of Honshu. Honshu is the largest of the four main islands that make up Japan. Iga and Koga were the places on Honshu where the first ninjas began to practice their secret skills.

Iga and Koga were melting pots of different cultures and ideas. During the 500s and 600s, China had undergone political disorder. Many people left China during this time and settled

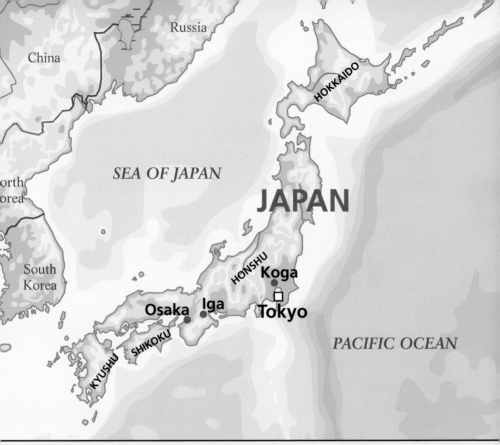

Honshu, called the mainland of Japan, is believed to be the birthplace of the mysterious ninja.

in Iga and Koga. Among those who came to Honshu were monks and military leaders.

These newcomers shared their Chinese philosophies and fighting skills with their new neighbors. The Chinese were exposed to the ways of Honshu as well. The techniques and way of life of the ninjas grew out of this mingling of skills and ideas.

## The Power of Nature

Many people who lived in Iga and Koga believed in the power of nature. They thought that humans could tap into the natural energy of the land. This was believed to make them physically and spiritually stronger. They also believed that people could learn to survive better in their world by understanding their physical surroundings.

One group of people who believed in the power of nature was called the *Shugenja*. They believed in putting themselves in dangerous situations. They thought this would help them overcome their personal fears. They also thought it would allow a person to take on the powers of nature. Walking through fire was one of the dangers the *Shugenja* put themselves through. Many historians believe that early ninjas borrowed some of the *Shugenja* beliefs in their training.

### FIGHTING WORDS

Ninjas study *ninjutsu*, which means "the art of stealth." It also describes the ninja's way of life. Today, *ninjutsu* refers to a certain style of martial arts that is based on ninja fighting techniques and beliefs.

## Attack on the Ninjas

Japanese warlords and samurai often mistreated ninjas. This was probably because ninjas followed different religious beliefs and military codes of behavior. To protect themselves, ninjas began to take action against the warlords and samurai. They sometimes disguised themselves as monks or peddlers to move about secretly. This allowed them to gather information about their enemies. Seeing how effective the ninjas were against them, warlords soon began hiring ninjas! These warlords used ninjas to spy on their enemies.

Taking on the identity of a monk or a peddler, such as this basket merchant, was an important survival skill for the ninja.

# CHAPTER TWO

# Learning the Art of Stealth

## Family Traditions

Ninjas were organized into clans. A clan was a group of families that joined together. Older members of a clan or family usually trained a ninja. Each clan had its own tradition, or style, of training. At one time, there were about seventy ninja clans in Koga and Iga.

## Training

Ninja training started at an early age. When they were about six years old, boys began playing games that required balance and quickness. They performed activities such as

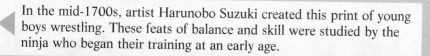

In the mid-1700s, artist Harunobo Suzuki created this print of young boys wrestling. These feats of balance and skill were studied by the ninja who began their training at an early age.

17

> ### THREE CLASSES OF NINJA
>
> Most clans had three classes of ninja. The ninja boss in a clan was called the *jonin*. He made the decision about who his ninjas would work for. Few ninjas knew who their *jonin* was because he used middlemen to deliver his orders. These middlemen were called *chunin*. Many *chunin* were also responsible for selecting the right ninja for the right job. The field agents were called the *genin*. It is the *genin's* feats that have inspired many of the astonishing tales of the ninjas.

leaping over low bushes. As a student got older, the training became more challenging. Students began to study striking and kicking techniques. Exercises and movements that built strength were also practiced until they could be done perfectly. Other exercises helped stretch the student's muscles and joints.

Ninjas even trained to walk in different ways so that they would not be easily seen. Learning how to use a small, stabbing step allowed the ninja to move silently through shallow water or dry leaves. Sideways walking helped a ninja move quietly in the shadows of buildings or in tight passages. A sweeping step was used to help a ninja cross wooden planks or straw matting.

A ninja practices kicking techniques as a part of his unarmed fighting system called *dakentaijutsu* (dah-kehn-tye-jooht-sooh).

A ninja also trained his mind. A well-trained ninja used his powers of concentration to perform amazing physical feats. For example, ninjas were trained to dislocate their shoulders from their sockets. This allowed them to escape after being captured and tied up by an enemy. Some ninjas were even able to dislocate their jaws. This prevented them from telling important information to a foe.

## Weapons of Choice

Ninjas used a variety of weapons. One popular weapon was a wooden staff—a simple, yet deadly tool in a ninja's hands. A staff was usually between 3 and 6 feet (1 to 2 meters) long. Some ninja staffs were built to shoot poison-tipped darts.

Another popular weapon was the *shuriken*,

### FIGHTING WORDS

Although most ninjas were male, there were female ninjas. These ninjas were called *kunoichi*. *Kunoichi* were especially good as spies because most men did not expect women to be doing such dangerous work.

or the hand-hidden blade. A *shuriken* is a sharp-edged metal blade that is thrown at an opponent. *Shuriken* can be round, square, or star-shaped.

The *shuko*, or climbing claws, was another favorite. *Shuko* are metal bands with several curved spikes on one side. A ninja would slip a *shuko* over each of his hands and use the claws to climb trees or scale walls. *Shuko* could also be used as weapons to defend against a knife or a sword.

The *shinobi-zue*, or ninja cane, looked like an ordinary walking stick. However, it was

hollowed out to hide a variety of fighting tools. Some canes contained hidden knives or metal chains. Some of them were even used as blowguns to shoot darts.

The ninja used two types of throwing blades, or *shuriken*. The first type was straight. The second type (shown above) had many points and came in a variety of shapes.

The swords used by ninjas were usually shorter than the heavy swords used by samurai. A lighter, smaller sword allowed a ninja to move quickly and to fight in small spaces. A ninja kept his sword in a scabbard, or holder. The scabbard was often longer than the sword. The ninja could use this extra space to hide secret papers, poisons, or other weapons. Some scabbards were made so that they could be used as breathing tubes. These scabbards had removable tips. When a ninja needed to

Ninjas often used a *ninjato*, or ninja short sword, to fight.

hide underwater, he used his scabbard to breathe! He put one end of his scabbard in his mouth. The other end stuck out of the water, allowing him to get air.

## Body Blows

Ninjas were also masters of unarmed combat. This type of combat is called *taijutsu*. There are two different kinds of *taijutsu*.

One type of unarmed combat is called *dakentaijutsu* (dah-kehn-tye-jooht-sooh). It is the art of strikes, blocks, and kicks. Strikes are usually made with the hand. They can also be made with the head, knee, elbow, or other body parts.

A second type of unarmed combat is *jutaijutsu*. This technique uses locks, holds, throws, and chokes. *Jutaijutsu* allowed a ninja to grab an opponent in a way that prevented escape. Ninjas were also meant to use their bodies to throw or flip opponents to the ground. This style of fighting allowed a smaller person to defeat a larger opponent.

Ninja fighting style used striking and grabbing techniques together. The training was done as full-force fighting to teach realistic combat skills.

## Magical Powers?

Many myths claim that ninjas had magical powers. Ninjas did not have such powers. They were ordinary human beings. It was their special training and unusual way of fighting that often seemed magical to opponents.

Ninjas often used herbs and powders to produce effects that *seemed* magical. Some ninjas used special powders that stung the eyes. A ninja could throw this powder at an enemy. While the opponent was blinded by the powder, the ninja could run away. To his opponent, it seemed as if the ninja had disappeared into thin air!

Even before going on a mission, ninjas often cleverly planned their escape routes. This also contributed to the idea that the ninja had magical powers. Sometimes a ninja would dig a hole in the ground and hide there after the mission was completed. The ninja would jump into his pre-dug hole and cover himself with dirt. People chasing him would think he had vanished.

Understanding and blending in with his natural surroundings was another way that ninjas seemed supernatural to others. For example, some ninjas could roll themselves up into balls. In the dark of night, they could look like large rocks on the ground. Their enemies would be puzzled and frightened by the ninja's sudden disappearance.

## Secrets of a Ninja House

Most ninja houses looked like an average
farmhouse. However, inside they were filled
with secret passages and hidden spaces.
Ninjas hid weapons and important documents
in these secret places. Some ninja houses even
had entire hidden rooms built into them!
Secret ladders and tunnels were also built into
many ninja houses. Ninjas could use the
ladders and tunnels to quickly escape an enemy.

Ninjas often set up an "alarm" system
around their houses to warn them of people
outside. A ninja attached bells to thread and
strung the thread around his house. The
thread was also attached to bells inside the
house. When a person outside brushed against
the thread, it rang the bells inside the house.
This alerted the ninja to a possible threat
from an unwanted visitor.

The special houses of the ninja were equipped with many traps and secrets.

# CHAPTER THREE

# Warriors and Spies

Ninjas were very clever warriors. They used a variety of methods to attack, confuse, and annoy their enemies—doing whatever they could to defeat an opponent.

## Siege Warfare

Ninjas often engaged in siege warfare. In siege warfare, an army surrounds a place such as a city or a castle to prevent supplies from reaching it. The army then waits for those inside to surrender. A warlord's army would often lay siege to a castle after a small force of ninjas made a surprise attack. Ninjas would sneak

Places such as Himeji Castle needed to be protected from enemy attacks. Himeji Castle had many safeguards, including both inner and outer moats.

into a castle at night and set fires. While the enemy was busy fighting the fires, the warlord's army attacked from outside. Surrounded by a warlord's soldiers and with ninjas prowling within the castle, the enemy usually surrendered.

## The Eyes of a Spy

Spying was a skill used by many ninjas. A favorite technique was to slip unnoticed into an enemy army camp to gather information. A ninja could disguise himself as a monk in order to move through the camp. Another might hide in tall grass outside a camp. Once the ninja obtained the information he needed, he reported it to his commander. This information could include how many soldiers were in the camp or what kind of weapons they had.

A ninja was sometimes required to change his entire lifestyle when he was on an assignment. Sometimes a ninja might have to take on a new identity and live in an enemy community. For example, he might open a

The ninja needed more than a disguise to appear to be someone else. To pass himself off as a monk, for instance, a ninja would need to know all the customs and behaviors of a monk.

shop or become a farmer. The ninja could live for months or even years among the enemy. During this time, he secretly gave information about the community to his commanders.

A ninja would also pass false information to the enemy on purpose. One way this was done was by allowing enemy agents to "discover" false information that was supposed to be important. Thinking the information they discovered was true, the enemy might take actions that would play into the hands of the ninja. Some ninjas even acted as double agents. This meant that they pretended to be on the enemy's side. In fact, the ninja was still loyal to his master.

## A Dangerous Profession

Ninjas lived in constant danger. No matter how well trained or clever a ninja was, he was still at risk of being discovered. If a ninja was captured, he often faced a horrifying fate. Since he would not freely give up important information, his enemy would torture him. Among the tortures a ninja faced was having the skin stripped from his body. Another cruel torture was having all the bones in his body broken. Some enemies would even boil a ninja alive in oil or water. Knowing these horrors awaited him, a ninja often took his own life if he could not escape capture.

The ninja used a variety of skills to slip into an enemy stronghold. Once inside, the ninja could attack with fire or explosives, set traps, or poison his enemy's food or water. ▶

## Ninja Assassins

In a place where warlords battled each other for control of land, one common method of gaining more land was to kill a rival warlord. Sometimes a ninja was hired to kill his master's enemy. Once again, the ninja relied on his special training in the arts of secrecy and stealth to do his job. A ninja might attack an enemy who was traveling alone on a road. Another method that ninjas used was to lie among dead soldiers on a battlefield. When the enemy rode past, the ninja would jump up and attack him.

# CHAPTER FOUR

# The End of the Ninjas

## The Defeat of the Iga Ninjas

In the late 1500s, Japan began to undergo political and social changes. These changes led to the end of the ninjas in both Iga and Koga.

Oda Nobunaga was one of the most powerful warlords in Japan. He is known for ending the fighting between warlords. During the 1570s and early 1580s, he and his forces waged many bloody battles. Among his enemies were the ninjas. The exact reasons for this are not known. However, a tale tells of a day when Nobunaga was out hunting and his horse threw him. When Nobunaga landed on the ground, he felt he was being watched. He grew fearful, although he did not see anyone. He believed

The ninjas weren't the only ones destroyed by Oda Nobunaga. Nobunaga defeated this general from Akechi Mitsuhide's army in the late 1500s.

that there were ninjas nearby. He quickly rode away but he never forgot his fear of the ninjas. He decided to get rid of the ninjas once and for all. Nobunaga and his army attacked Iga to destroy the ninjas there. Nobunaga's army won the battle. Most of Iga's ninjas were killed. The survivors fled to other parts of Japan. From that time on, ninjas no longer lived or trained in Iga.

## Tokugawa Ieyasu and the Ninjas

The Koga ninjas experienced a different fate. A warlord named Tokugawa Ieyasu hired a group of Koga ninjas to work for him. In 1600, the Koga ninjas fought in the Battle of Sekigahara. This was the largest battle ever fought in Japan. The ninjas engaged in siege warfare against opposing warlords. Ieyasu won the battle, allowing him to become shogun.

In about 1638, a group of farmers rebelled against their local leader because he treated them cruelly. Their revolt was called the Shimabara Rebellion. As the rebellion grew stronger, Ieyasu worried that it was a threat to his rule. He sent his army and a group of ninjas

This statue of Tokugawa Ieyasu stands in Nikko National Park in Japan.

to fight the farmers. The ninjas slipped into a castle called Hara and gathered information about how it was built. They also learned where the enemy soldiers and the weapons were. Ninjas also stole food and supplies from the castle. Meanwhile, Ieyasu's army laid siege to the castle from outside its walls. The siege lasted for many weeks. Finally, the rebels inside Hara gave up. The rebellion was over.

## The End of an Era

The Shimabara Rebellion was the last major battle in which ninjas played an important part. After 1638, Japan was at peace. Without a need for their military service, the ninjas' way of life was over. Instead, they became ordinary citizens. Over the years, many ninjas found jobs as farmers, tradesmen, teachers, policemen, or security agents. Some became outlaws or criminals. Finally, in 1868, all government-run ninja schools were closed. Several ninja masters continued to teach the old skills over the next few decades, but the days of the ninja warrior had come to an end.

## Gone, but Not Forgotten

As years passed, stories of the ninjas' strength and skill became part of Japanese culture. These stories often included fantastic elements such as the use of magical powers. In some stories, ninjas were able to turn themselves into animals. Other stories talked of ninjas as beings who could fly or disappear into thin air. Ninjas also appeared in Kabuki, a type of Japanese theater. Ninjas appeared in works of art, too.

After World War II, Japanese moviemakers began using the legends and history of the ninjas in their films. This helped create a worldwide

This is a Kabuki actor performing in full costume. Kabuki is a popular form of Japanese theater.

**FIGHTING WORDS**

Some people believe that Japan used ninjas during World War II (1939–1945).

interest in the skills and accomplishments of Japan's ancient warriors. Ninja characters have appeared in hundreds of movies and TV shows. They are also frequently featured in video games and are the heroes of countless books and comic books. Ninjas have even been the subject of children's cartoons, such as the Teenage Mutant Ninja Turtles.

Japan's ninja warriors were feared as legendary spies and assassins, ready to strike an opponent at a moment's notice. They were masters of the martial arts. They were experts at the use of unusual weapons. Their skills and methods made them seem supernatural to the people of ancient Japan. Yet although little remains of their old ways in our modern world, they are still remembered and respected as powerful and mysterious warriors of the past.

Legends of the ninjas' stealth and trickery have made them one of the most feared figures in Japanese history.

# New Words

**assassins** (uh-**sass**-uhnz) people who murder someone else

**dislocate** (diss-**loh**-kate) to move something out of its original place

**feudalism** (**fyoo**-duh-li-zuhm) the medieval system in which people were given land and protection by the landowner, or lord, in return for working and fighting

**Kabuki** (kuh-**boo**-kee) a type of Japanese drama traditionally performed by men in elaborate costumes

**lethal** (lee-thuhl) harmful enough to kill

**martial arts** (**mar**-shuhl **arts**) styles of fighting or self-defense that come mainly from the Far East

**moats** (**mohts**) a deep, wide ditch dug all around a castle or fort and filled with water to prevent attacks

**ninja** (**nin**-juh) a person who is highly trained in ancient Japanese martial arts, especially one hired as a spy or assassin

# New Words

**rebellion** (ri-**bel**-yuhn) an armed fight against a government

**samurai** (**sam**-oo-rye) a Japanese warrior who lived in medieval times

**scabbard** (**skab**-urd) a case that holds a sword, dagger, or bayonet when it is not in use

**scale** (**skale**) to climb up something

**shogun** (**show**-gunn) the title given to the military leader of Japan from the twelfth to the nineteenth centuries

**siege** (**seej**) the surrounding of a place such as a city or a castle to cut off supplies and then wait for those inside to surrender

**stealth** (**stelth**) to act in a secret and quiet manner

**technique** (tek-**neek**) a method or way of doing something that requires skill, as in the arts, sports, or sciences

# For Further Reading

Chaline, Eric, and Aidan Trimble. *Ninjutsu*. Broomall, PA: Mason Crest Publishers, 2002.

Hall, Eleanor J. *Life among the Samurai*. Farmington Hills, MI: Gale Group, 1998.

Kimmel, Eric A. *Sword of the Samurai: Adventure Stories from Japan*. New York: HarperCollins Children's Books, 2000.

MacDonald, Fiona, and David Antram. *A Samurai Castle*. New York: McGraw-Hill Children's Publishing, 2001.

# Resources

## Organizations

**Asia Society**
725 Park Avenue
New York, NY 10021
(212) 288-6400
http://www.asiasociety.org

**The Metropolitan Museum of Art**
Arms and Armor (Permanent Exhibit)
1000 Fifth Avenue
New York, New York 10028
(212) 535-7710
http://www.metmuseum.org

# RESOURCES

## Web Sites

### Enter the Ninja
*http://www.entertheninja.com/*
This Web site explains how ninjas were trained
and what techniques they used in battle.

### Ninja Kids
*http://www.winjutsu.com*
This excellent Web site is packed with information
on a variety of topics. It includes a history of the
ninja, descriptions of weapons and fighting
techniques, and special stories and activities
for kids.

### Tenshin Dojo–History of the Ninja
*http://www.genbukan.no/index.php?id=&lang=en*
This very informative Web site includes information
about the ninja's history and the weapons they used.
There are also links to other sites and pictures
from Japan.

# Index

# Index

## About the Author

Joanne Mattern is the author of more than one hundred nonfiction books for children. Joanne lives in New York State with her husband, two daughters, and several cats.